Chinese Brush Painting

for Beginners

CHINESE BRUSH PAINTING

THE VANGUARD PRESS, INC.   NEW YORK

for Beginners

by
VICKEY AUBREY

Designed by Elizabeth Woll

Library of Congress Cataloging in Publication Data

Aubrey, Vickey.
   Chinese brush painting for beginners.
   Designed by Elizabeth Woll.

   Bibliography: p.
   Summary: An introduction to the basic techniques of the ancient art of
Chinese brush painting, including the strokes needed to paint the bamboo, fish,
plum blossom, and six other subjects.
   1. Brush drawing—Technique—Juvenile literature.   2. Water-color
painting, Chinese—Juvenile literature.   [1. Brush drawing—
Technique.   2. Watercolor painting—Technique]   I. Title.
ND2460.A9   1981   751.42′51   81-19651
ISBN 0-8149-0851-9   AACR2

Table of Contents

Introduction

This book is about a new way of learning to paint. You probably learned to paint in school. The paper and paints were handed to you and your teacher told you to paint a tree, a house, a flower, or whatever you wanted. Having the opportunity to put your own ideas down on paper is an excellent way of discovering art. But have you ever noticed that you were never told how to paint these objects? And if you asked for help in painting, you were usually told to use your imagination. Our culture stresses creativity rather than the techniques of painting.

But art is not always thought of or taught the same way in all cultures. In this book you will learn the art of Chinese Brush Painting.

Brush painting began 1400 years ago in the world's oldest civilization. A man named Hsieh Ho developed six canons (rules) for painting that are still followed by brush painters today. You will only need to understand one of these canons in order to learn the basic techniques of brush painting. This canon is: "Study by copying the old masters." Old masters are past expert brush painters. Copying the paintings of others makes it possible to pass down the rules and techniques from generation to generation. The brush painter learns the techniques by copying, but his painting is unique in that it expresses his own personality.

Brush painting celebrates the wonders of nature. The brush painter does not paint from a model. He studies the subject, then returns to paint the image from memory. It is necessary for the artist to have a very steady hand, for the painting is done in quick smooth movements. No erasing or painting over is allowed, so mastering the strokes is very important.

Besides the six canons, the artist is only allowed to paint the following subjects:

    (1) landscapes
    (2) portraits and human figures
    (3) flowers and birds
    (4) bamboo and stones
    (5) animals
    (6) palaces and other buildings

In this book you will learn the basic brush strokes needed to paint a fish, baby chick, kitten, bamboo, plum blossom, cat, mouse, fruit, and butterfly. When you feel you can paint these subjects well, take a look at the animals and insects you see every day. Study one of them and try using the brush strokes to paint its basic shape. Remember, learning the basic strokes of brush painting can be relaxing, so enjoy yourself.

I·Traditional Materials

Before World War II, brush painting was done in black ink. Painting with black ink is sometimes called *sumie,* which is the name of the black ink stick the artist uses.

Pictured on the following pages are the materials the brush painter uses. Since these materials are hard to find and expensive, I have listed everyday materials you may use. Most of these materials may be purchased at any store that sells art supplies, or you may already have them around the house.

INK STICK

When the phrase "black ink" is mentioned to us, we immediately picture a black liquid. It is not common for us to think of it in any other form. In China, however, ink comes in a small dry rectangle and is called an ink stick. The ink stick is made from the soot (a black substance that remains when something is burned) of burned pine wood and a glue made from fish. This mixture is poured into a rectangular mold and placed in a small room made of sweet-smelling sandalwood to harden. These sticks are usually decorated with pictures or Chinese calligraphy (writing).

INKSTONE

The inkstone can be made from many different materials, but the most popular are the ones made from slate. Rectangular-shaped inkstones are sold in art stores here but they are actually made in many varieties of shapes in China. At one end of the stone is a well (the deeper end of the stone).

INK

To make the ink you put two teaspoons of water in the well. Now take the ink stick and dip one end into the well. Slide the stick up to the flat surface of the stone and rub it in a circular motion. You

Ink stick

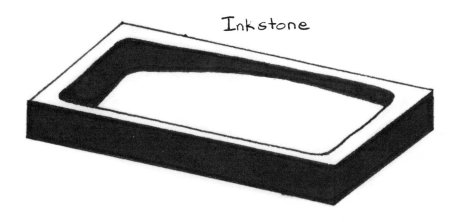

Inkstone

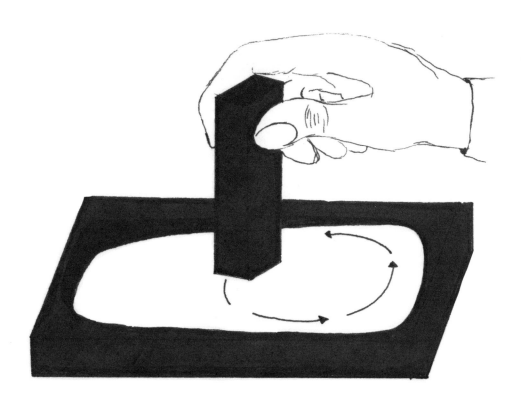

have to make about 400 circles before the ink is ready to use. The brush painter uses the task of grinding the ink for putting himself into a quiet, calm mood for painting.

BRUSHES

The Chinese brushes are made from bamboo and soft or hard animal hairs. A variety of sharply pointed and thick brushes are needed to make all the brush-painting strokes. The artist is very careful with his brushes and keeps them for a lifetime. You can take care of your brushes in the same way. Wash your brushes carefully when you are finished and never use hot water, because it may melt the glue holding the bristles together.

PAPER

Paper was invented in China back in 105 A.D. by a man named Ts'ai Lun. Before paper was invented, the brush painter used beautiful silks. Many of the better brush-painting artists today still paint on silk, but it is too expensive for the beginner. The paper we use is usually made from wood or rags. Brush-painting paper can be made from rice, straw, hemp, linen, and the rice-paper tree. If you want to buy brush-painting paper here, ask for rice paper; but remember, not all the paper is actually rice paper.

You have probably seen artists in this country painting on an easel or a slanted table. The brush painter uses a flat-surfaced table and a small weight resting at the top of the paper to hold it down. Just as easel painters stand, so do brush painters. Standing allows them to move their arms freely for the larger strokes. Remember, they cannot paint over or erase any strokes. They need plenty of moving space to make the strokes right the first time.

2· Materials You Need

INK

Black watercolor or India ink works well for the beginning brush painter. Watercolor is the most practical to use because it washes easily out of your clothes.

BRUSHES

You will need two brushes, a small pointed one and an average-sized one. The brush that comes with your watercolors is a good size for your larger brush. Judge the size of the brushes you will need by the ones pictured.

PAPER

Use old newspapers for your practice paper at the beginning. Since you won't be saving these first attempts, it's a cheap way to practice. Once you have mastered some of the strokes, you will want better paper. Buy a newsprint pad that is inexpensive and very absorbent.

India Ink

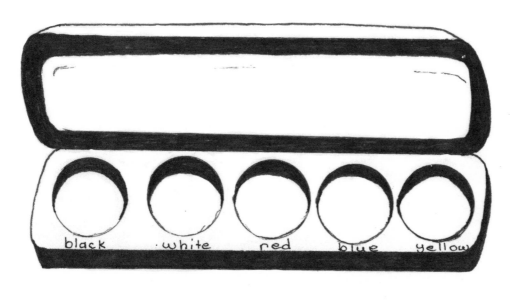

black   white   red   blue   yellow

News print

OTHER ITEMS NEEDED

You will need sheets of old newspaper for placing under your paper. These will absorb some of the water so your painting will not spread all over the page. Paper towels will also help absorb some of the water. Blot your brushes on the towels before using them. Now find three or four small bowls for mixing your shades of black ink or watercolor and you are ready to begin.

PREPARATION

Spread out plenty of newspaper on a flat table. Place your drawing paper to one side of you and your materials to the other. It is important that you can reach everything easily. Tear off a few paper towels and fold them neatly. This will be your blotter, so make it about three or four layers thick.

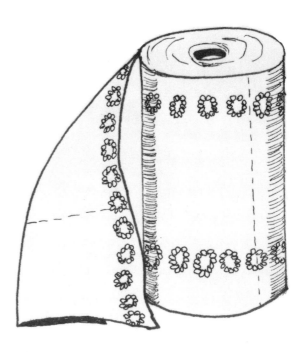

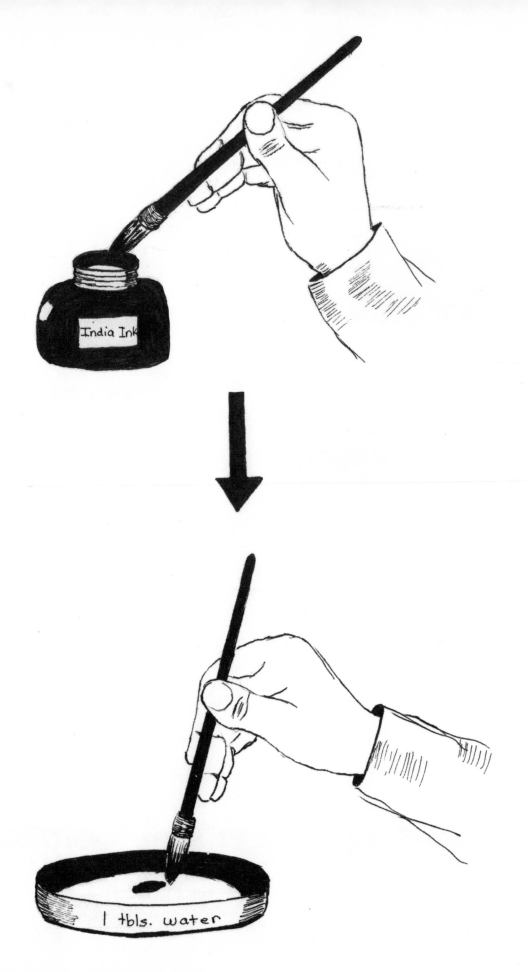

India Ink

1 tbls. water

Now you are ready to prepare your shades of black ink. Fill one of the bowls with clear water. If you have four bowls you can pour some of the black ink into one of the bowls. This is much easier than dipping your brush into the ink bottle. With watercolors you don't need a fourth bowl. All you have to do is touch the water-color with the tip of a wet brush for a dark black shade.

In the other two bowls you will need to mix a medium and a light shade of black.

To mix these shades, start with one tablespoon of water and a brush full of black ink. Stir this mixture lightly with your brush and blot the brush on a clean piece of white paper. Now you can see what shade of black you have made.

 clear water

 Black

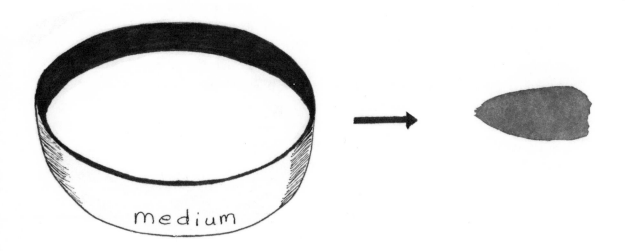 medium

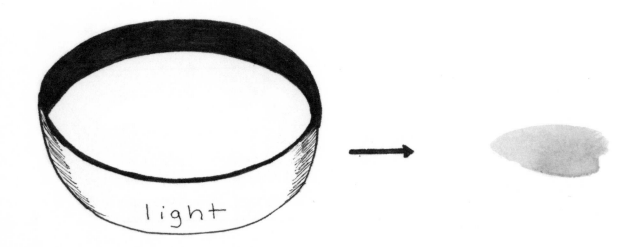 light

Check the shade of black you have made with the sample shades next to the medium and light bowls on this page. Keep adding either black or clear water until your shades are close to the ones on the opposite page.

3· Brush Strokes

THE THREE-INK STROKE

The most amazing stroke in brush painting is the three-ink stroke. You can actually paint three different shades of black in one brush stroke. In order for this to be possible the brush has to contain all three shades. It is actually very simple to do. Just follow the next three steps.

Soak the whole brush in the light ink. Hold it over the bowl a few seconds to let some of the ink drip out. After this you can blot it lightly on the paper towels.

Light

Now put about one-half of the brush in the medium ink. Again hold the brush over the bowl for a few seconds and blot lightly.

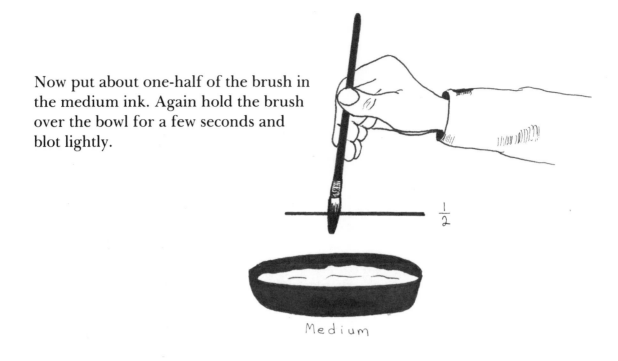

Medium

Just lightly touch the tip to the dark ink and you are ready to make the three-ink stroke.

Tip

Dark

But before you actually begin making the brush strokes, you need to learn the proper way of holding a brush for brush painting.

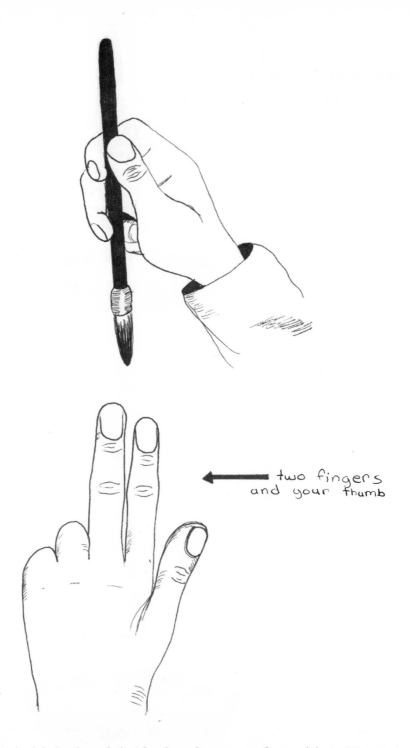

two fingers and your thumb

First, hold the brush in the hand you use for writing. Your thumb, middle, and index fingers are the only ones touching the brush. Try holding the brush as pictured above. A good way to find out if you are holding it correctly is to place an egg in your palm at the same time. If the egg feels secure you are ready to begin brush painting.

THE WIDE THREE-INK STROKE

Prepare your brush for the three-ink stroke. Now hold your brush firmly, with the bristles pushed flat on the paper. Pull the brush straight across the page, then lift it up quickly. Your stroke should be dark across the top and light across the bottom, as in the illustration. Practice making straight lines like these across your paper. When your straight lines begin to look right, try making circles and curves. You want to make sure you are using your whole arm for the strokes and not just your wrist. When you are no longer aware of the brush in your hand, you are on your way to becoming a brush painter.

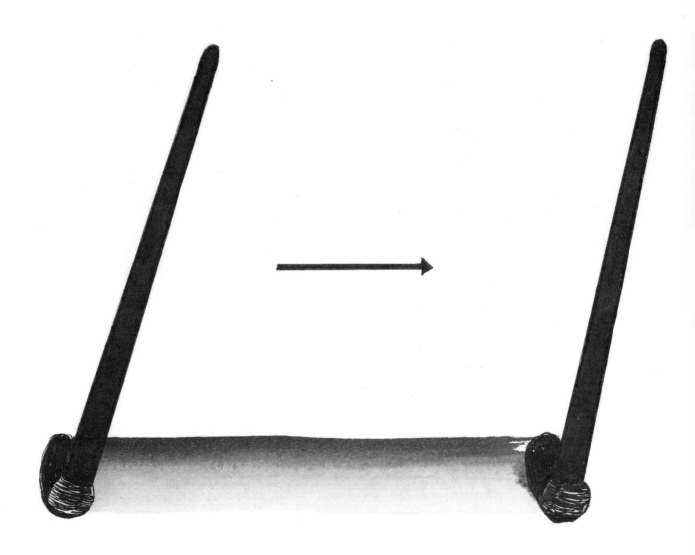

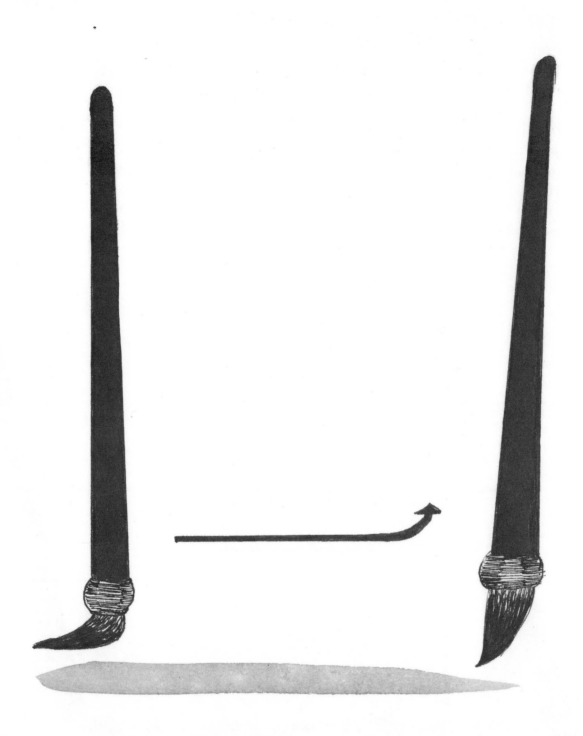

PULLING STROKE

Place your brush flat on the paper again. This time you want to make a short, quick, pulling stroke. Lift the brush up quickly so that the tip makes a point at the end of the stroke.

DOT STROKE

This is a very simple stroke that you probably use every time you paint. All you have to do is to touch the tip of the brush to the paper.

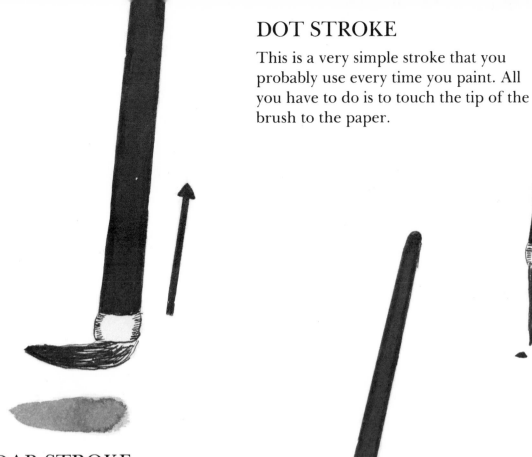

DAB STROKE

Fill your brush with any shade of ink, then push the brush down on the paper. Lift it quickly and you have the dab stroke.

FINE LINE

Practice this stroke until you can make a very straight, fine line. Now practice all the strokes until you find them very easy to make.

4 · The Fish

In making the body of the fish, you will need to prepare your brush as you did for the three-ink stroke. The body stroke of the fish is your basic *pulling stroke*.

Touch the tip of your brush to the front of the fish and make a short, slanted stroke.

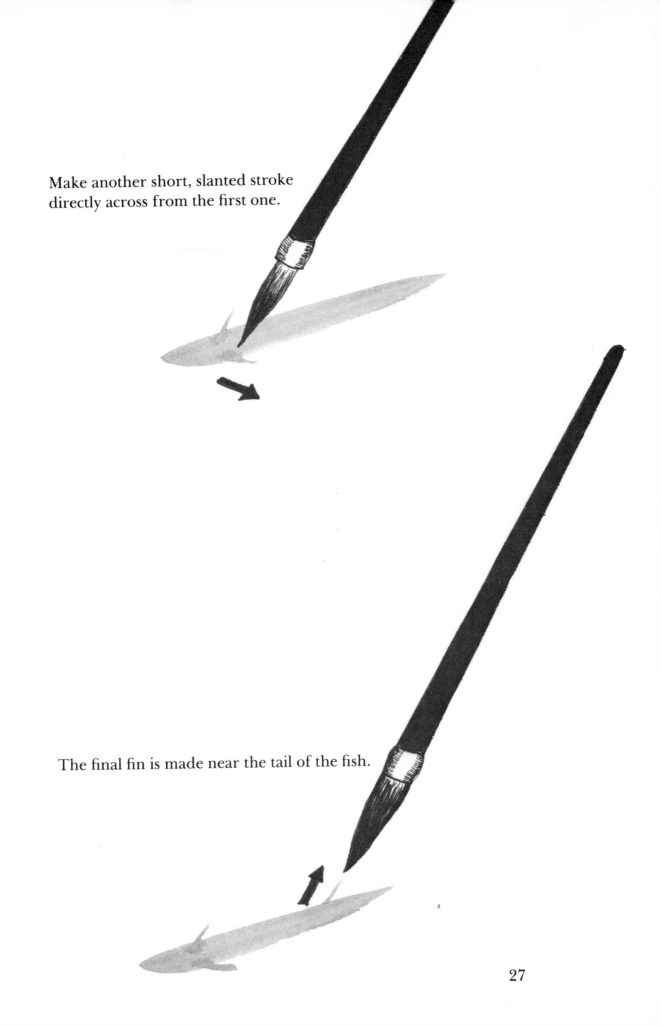

Make another short, slanted stroke directly across from the first one.

The final fin is made near the tail of the fish.

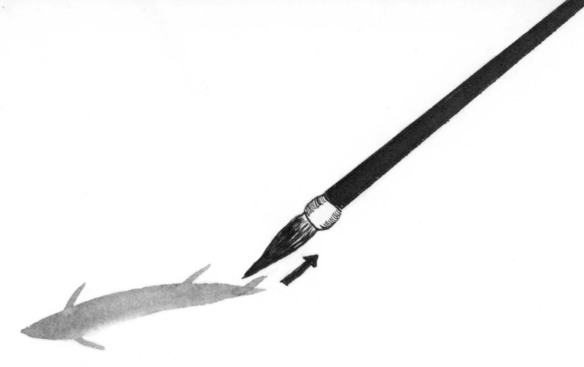

For the tail, make a short stroke next to the point of the fish body.

The nose is made by painting two fine lines at the front of the fish. Now clean your brush and dip the tip in the dark black ink. Blot it and paint a dot for the eye.

Now that you know how to paint the fish, you can make all sorts of underwater scenes. The brush painter does not paint everything he sees, as some artists do. Look at the picture above; you know the fish are swimming in water, but do you think it is necessary to paint the water? With a little imagination you can see an ocean or a lake in the picture.

Look at the picture again and you will notice that some of the fish are darker than others. The fish that are dark appear to be in front of the lighter fish. By experimenting with lightness and darkness in shading, you will come up with a very real-looking picture.

5·The Baby Chick

Spread your brush flat in the dark black ink and make a large dab stroke. If your brush is not large enough, you can make two dab strokes right next to each other.

Make three small dab strokes, again in black, directly behind the head. Try not to spread the strokes too far apart or you will end up with a very large chicken.

Paint in black a short, fine line toward the head for the beak.

The body stroke may seem difficult, but it is really very simple. All you are actually doing is making a wide number two around the back of the chick. Using the medium black, place your brush down at the top of the chick. The bristles should be flat. Pull the brush around as if you were making a two. Quickly lift the brush up off the paper when you have finished.

For this stroke you want to touch the tip of the brush to the base of the beak, using the medium black. Pull the brush downward, flattening it against the body as you go. This stroke may take some practice.

A baby chick has delicate legs, so try to paint the legs in black as finely as possible.

Wash out your brush and touch the tip to the black ink and make
the eye. With a little practice you will be able to make the baby
chick quickly.

6·The Kitten

You learned earlier that the brush painter does not paint everything he sees. The kitten is an excellent example of this. A few brush strokes placed in the correct places can be identified as a kitten. Since the whole kitten is not going to be painted, it is necessary to place the few strokes in the proper areas. You will be surprised at how much your finished product appears to be a kitten.

Imagine a kitten's face on the paper in front of you. You will find it much easier to place the ears in their proper position when you have succeeded in doing this. Use the medium ink and the dab stroke to paint the ears.

Using the medium ink again, paint two circles a little below the ears. Let the two circles dry. Now dab your smaller brush in the dark ink. Paint a fine line around each of the eyes.

Clean your small brush and fill it with the medium ink again. Place the tip of the brush at the beginning of the mouth. Pull the brush a little downward while putting more pressure on it. Quickly pull it back up, lifting the brush as you do. When you push harder on the brush, the line is much thicker than when you take the pressure off.

Clean your small brush again and dip it in the dark ink. Paint a curved line to the beginning of the right ear. This line is only about ½ inch in length. Now continue this line around the ear's outer edge to its top. Another line is then painted on the opposite side of the ear and is a bit shorter in length.

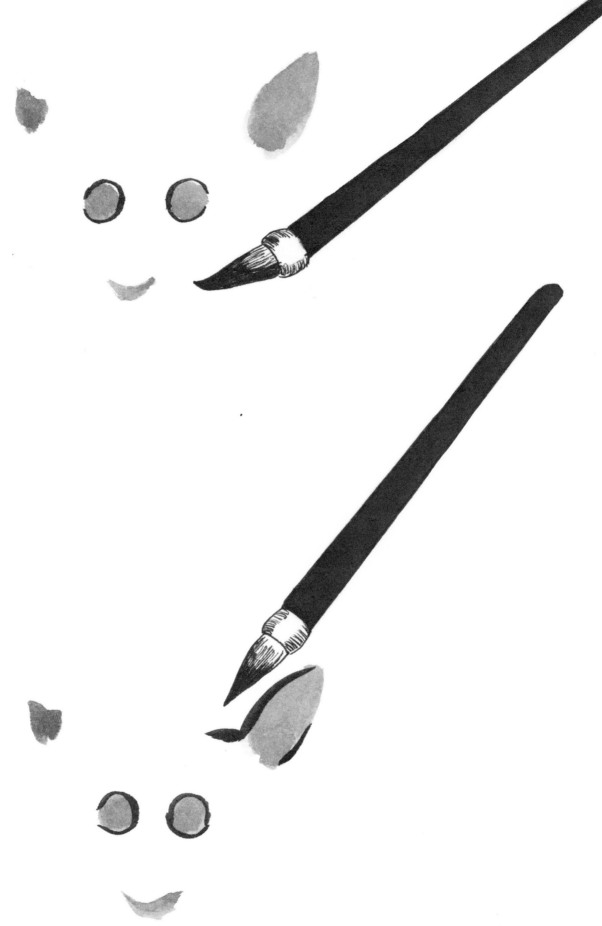

Take your large brush and fill it with medium ink. To paint the paws of the kitten you will be using the dab stroke. Sometimes this seems to be the easiest step in painting the kitten. The stroke may be easy, but placing the paws in the correct place is important and will take practice. Study the picture so that you can paint the strokes in the correct position.

Find the area that is directly above the middle of the rear paw and across from the bottom of the right ear. Place your large brush here to paint the tail. Press the brush while pulling it up and around, making the tail slightly curved. When you reach the end of the tail, lift the brush up to make the point.

1

2

3

For the finishing touch, paint four fine lines on either side of the face for whiskers.

Does this look like a kitten to you? The body may not be painted in, but you know that it is there.

7 · The Bamboo

The bamboo is one of the most popular subjects in brush painting. It can also be one of the most fun to paint. Since you are using the three-ink stroke, the bamboo stalks will appear to be three-dimensional. The shading on the left side of the bamboo stalk causes its rounded appearance.

Once you have learned all the steps to painting the bamboo, then every picture you create can be different. The bamboo can be painted in any thickness and is either three or five sections long.

Painting a section of the bamboo is almost the same as painting the three-ink stroke. However, this time push your brush upward instead of painting the stroke across the paper. When you arrive at the end of the stroke, lift the brush up and pull it off to the left of the stalk.

This stroke indicates the joints of each of the bamboo sections. Fill your small brush with dark ink. Paint a tiny dab stroke on the left side of the stalk. Now pull a fine line stroke across the stalk and end with another dab stroke. The bamboo stalks do not have to be completely dry to paint the joint. Some of the dark ink bleeding into the stalk adds more life to the bamboo.

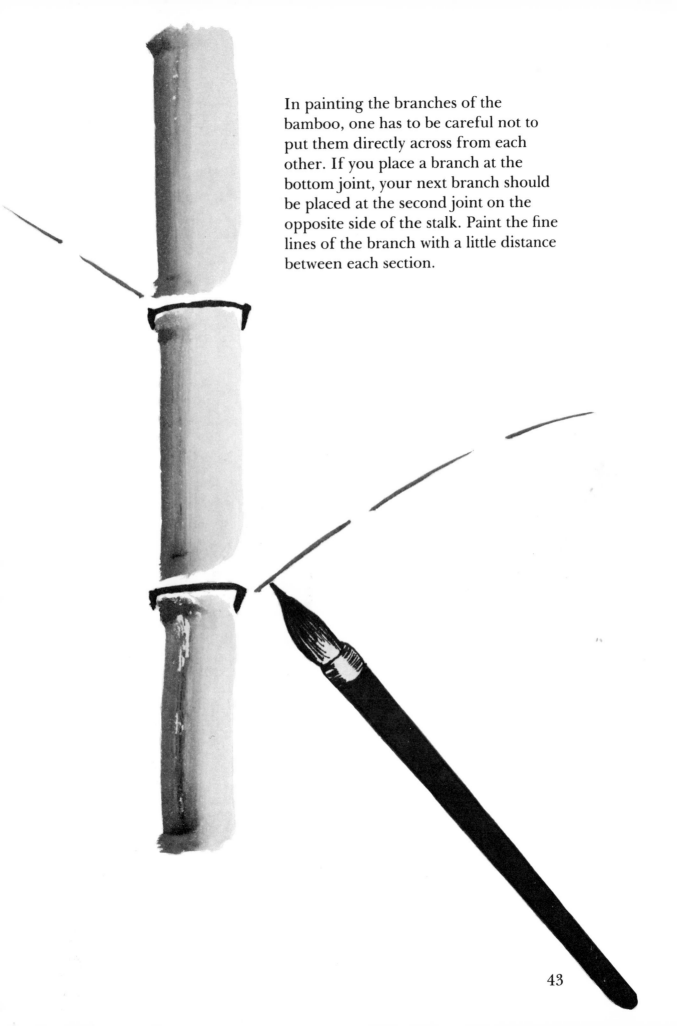

In painting the branches of the bamboo, one has to be careful not to put them directly across from each other. If you place a branch at the bottom joint, your next branch should be placed at the second joint on the opposite side of the stalk. Paint the fine lines of the branch with a little distance between each section.

The leaves are painted with the same stroke as the fish (pulling stroke). With practice you will be able to do these strokes very quickly.

As you can see, the sections of the bamboo can be wide or narrow. You are free to decide the width of the bamboo. However, there are traditional rules about the length. As we learned before, you can paint either three or five sections. The first sections should be shorter than the last ones. And the final section should be unfinished.

8·The Plum Blossom

The plum blossom is a very delicate flower that grows on an old, dead-looking branch. It is another favorite subject of the brush painter.

Using your small brush and medium ink, paint five connecting ovals.

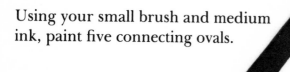

Let the petals dry a minute; then paint around eight fine lines from the center of the petals.

Paint small dots around the tops of these fine lines.

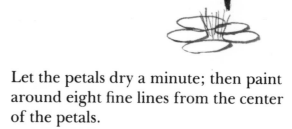

These are the plum-blossom buds and are painted with medium ink.

In painting the side or upside-down view of the plum blossom, the eight fine lines are no longer necessary. Just paint dots around the edges of the petals.

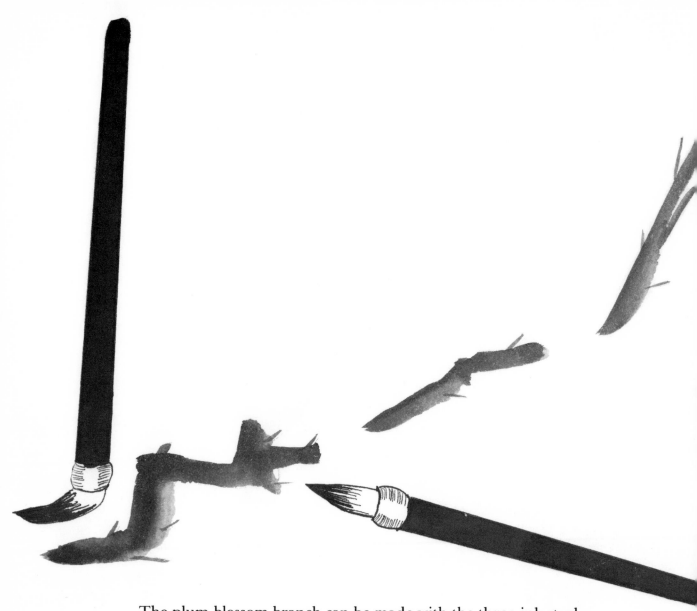

The plum-blossom branch can be made with the three-ink stroke or you can just use the two darker shades. Leave a few spaces for the flowers.

The many thorns can be made with fine line strokes. Place your brush on the branch and pull it up as quickly as possible.

To finish your picture, paint flowers in the spaces and along the edges of the branch. Use a variety of blossoms and buds.

9·The Cat

Fill your brush with medium ink, then blot most of the water out of it. The cat is made with a drier brush than you have been using. Push your brush against the paper as you bring it around to paint the head of the cat.

Using medium ink again, place two dab strokes on both sides of the head for the ears.

The head stroke is repeated in the
body of the cat. Only this time it will be
much larger.

The tail is made with a quick stroke
from the cat body. Lift the brush up at
the end so that it comes to a point.

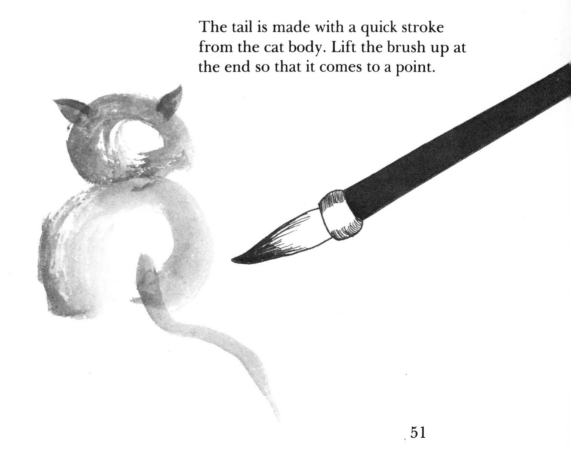

10 · The Mouse

Medium ink is used for the body of the mouse. Be sure your stroke is a long one. Take a look at a mouse and you will see that its body is quite a bit longer than its head.

Add a little dark ink to your brush and paint a dab stroke for the head.

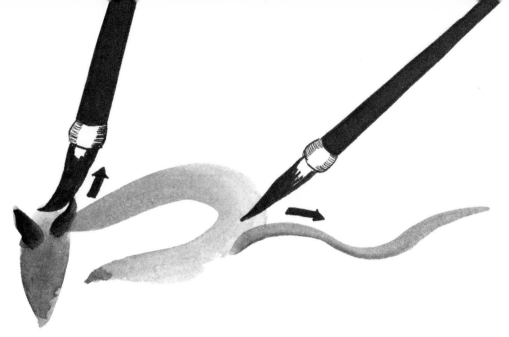

Let the head dry and then paint two small, dark ink strokes for the ears. The tail is similar to that of the cat, only it is a bit narrower.

Paint the letter *m* on both sides of the lower face. These strokes will run together. Don't worry about this because that is just what you want them to do.

1 2 3   4 5 6

Paint two dots for the eyes. Now clean the brush and dip it in medium ink. A soft line can be added across the back of the mouse for a little shading.

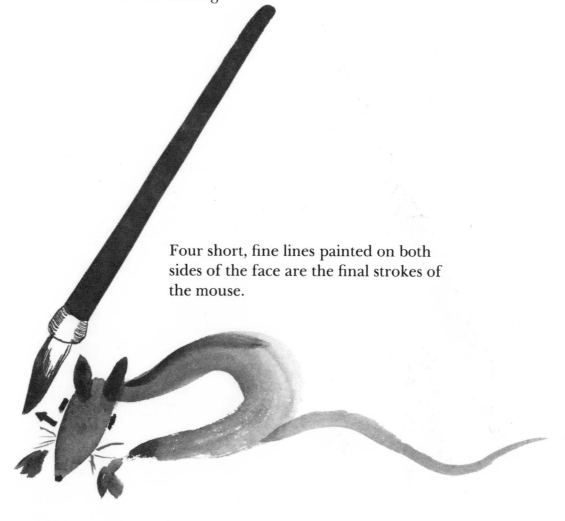

Four short, fine lines painted on both sides of the face are the final strokes of the mouse.

11 · Fruit

The stem is painted with the dark ink. Make a short fine line across the top of the paper. Now put some pressure on the brush and pull it downward. Lift it up quickly, for the stroke is very short.

These are dab strokes using the three-ink method of filling your brush. Make sure the third stroke is not placed too near the stem.

If you notice, the fruit is not made with one continuous stroke. Two medium ink strokes are used so that a space can be left at the bottom of the apple.

The space is left so that you can add another piece of fruit to the picture. By placing the fruit in this position it appears to be in front of the other piece.

12 · The Butterfly

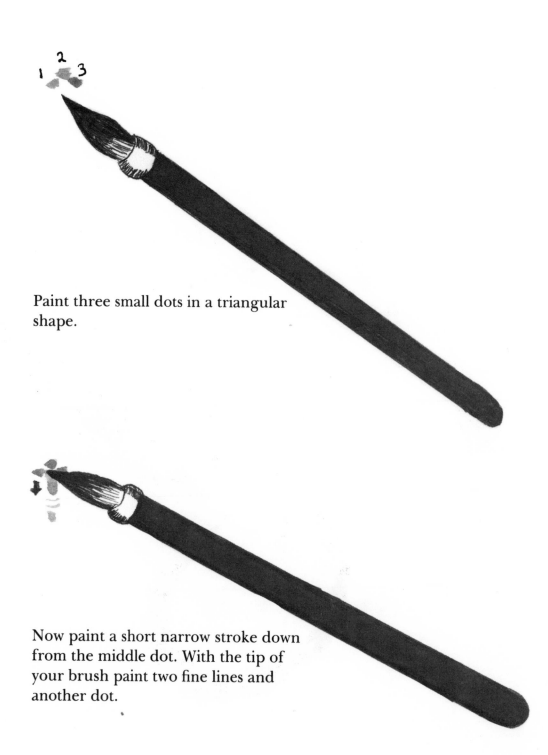

Paint three small dots in a triangular shape.

Now paint a short narrow stroke down from the middle dot. With the tip of your brush paint two fine lines and another dot.

Lay your brush to the side of the butterfly's body and pull inward.

Let the upper wings dry before painting the two lower ones. Place the brush next to the body and pull downward.

Place the antennae away from the head so the butterfly will appear to be in motion.

13 · Special Projects

MAKING WRAPPING PAPER

Save your practice sheets. They make excellent wrapping paper. If you're not happy with the results of your practice sheets, then design your own wrapping paper.

Take a large sheet of any colored paper. Make sure the paper doesn't tear easily or you will have difficulties later. You can either paint a pattern of one subject or combine any number of the subjects learned.

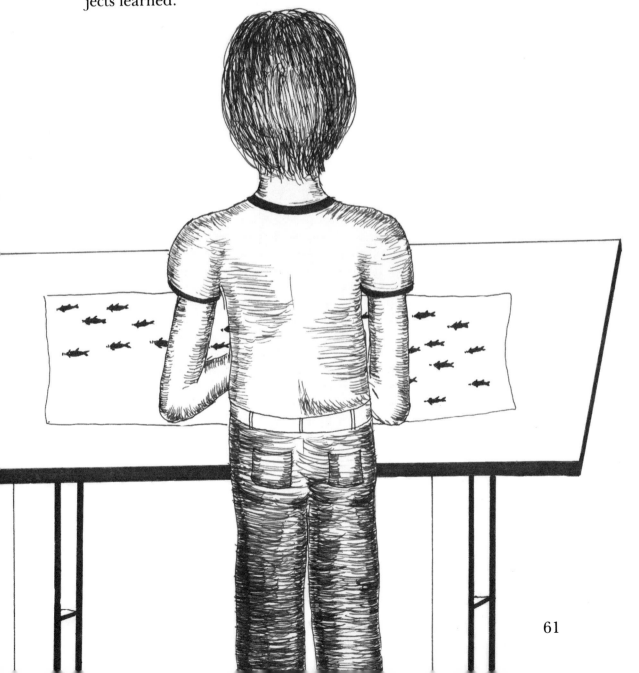

MAKING GREETING CARDS

Fold a large sheet of paper to the size you desire to make your card. Instead of cutting it, insert a dinner knife in the fold and pull it through the paper. This gives the paper an edge similar to that of rice paper. Paint any of the brush painting subjects you have learned on the outside of the card.

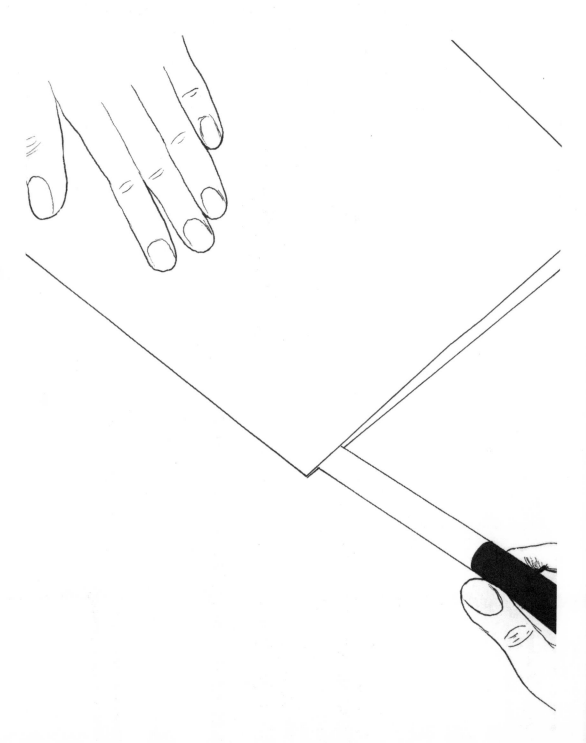

EXPERIMENTING WITH COLOR

Now that you have mastered the brush painting subjects in this book, try adding some color. The brush painter uses only the true colors of the subjects. You may want to experiment with colors and use all sorts of strange combinations. This can be a lot of fun, so enjoy yourself!

References

THE LIVELY ART OF INK PAINTING
   by Ryozo Ogura, Japan Publications Inc., 1968

JAPANESE BRUSH PAINTING IN COLOR
   by Kohei Aida, Japan Publications Inc., 1973

THE HOW AND WHY OF CHINESE PAINTING
   by Diana Kan, Van Nostrand Reinhold Company, 1974